Those *A-Ha* Moments

Spiritual Growth Through Journaling

Lynnette Goldy

PublishAmerica
Baltimore

© 2010 by Lynnette Goldy.
All rights reserved. No part of this book may be reproduced, stored in a retrieval system or transmitted in any form or by any means without the prior written permission of the publishers, except by a reviewer who may quote brief passages in a review to be printed in a newspaper, magazine or journal.

First printing

PublishAmerica has allowed this work to remain exactly as the author intended, verbatim, without editorial input.

This publication contains the opinions and ideas of its author. Author intends to offer information of a general nature. Any reliance on the information herein is at the reader's own discretion.

The author and publisher specifically disclaim all responsibility for any liability, loss, or right, personal or otherwise, which is incurred as a consequence, directly or indirectly, of the use and application of any contents of this book. They further make no representations or warranties with respect to the accuracy or completeness of the contents of this work and specifically disclaim all warranties including without limitation any implied warranty of fitness for a particular purpose. Any recommendations are made without any guarantee on the part of the author or the publisher.

Hardcover 978-1-4489-5896-2
Softcover 978-1-61546-709-9
PAperback 978-1-4512-4749-7
PUBLISHED BY PUBLISHAMERICA, LLLP
www.publishamerica.com
Baltimore

Printed in the United States of America

"Scripture taken from the NEW AMERICAN STA
BIBLE®, © Copyright 1960, 1962, 1963, 1968, 1971, 1972, 19
1977, 1995 by The Lockman Foundation Used by per
(www.Lockman.org) unless otherwise indicated by "KJV" (Ki
Version) which is public domain.

May You Listen To the Holy Spirit in Every Moment of Yo

Table of Contents

Introduction to the Author 7
Introduction to Journaling 9
The Opportunities for Journaling 14
    Prayer 14
    Reflection 27
    Christian Meditation 70
    Lectio Divina 82
Journal-ists 95
More Reflections 103
Epilogue 117
My Journey 121
Glossary 133

INTRODUCTION TO THE AUTHOR

I was born in 1952 in Colorado, the middle of three daughters, to parents who brought me up in the Christian faith. Our lives were not always idyllic, although looking back one could say we did at times resemble the Ozzie and Harriet Nelson family. Anyway, that's where my memory takes us. Our parents were married once and always to each other. As teenagers my sisters and I rebelled against the rules, and lived to tell about it (or not tell). Despite my walking down some fairly crooked roads, my two marriages (one divorce), and serious health issues in my family, Christ continues to reassure and encourage me, and He keeps me accountable.

My husband, Eric, is an Anglican pastor and we have two children and one grandchild. Three years ago Eric was diagnosed with chronic Lyme disease and amyotrophic lateral sclerosis (ALS), often referred to as "Lou Gehrig's Disease." Life has been difficult at times but Christ's love and the love of family and friends gets us through. Galatians 6:2 says, *"Bear one another's burdens, and thereby fulfill the law of Christ,"* which is love.

My church journey has been diverse. I grew up in the Disciples of Christ church where I learned about God: Father, Son and Holy Spirit and was baptized at the age of 12. I had great teachers and a church family. In my early twenties, I attended a Pentecostal church as well as a Foursquare Church. I became Episcopalian in my thirties. In my forties, I was drawn to the mystery of Christianity in the Greek Orthodox Church and was chrismated, taking on the name Stephania after both my father and St. Stephen. When I was fifty, Eric was ordained in the Anglican Mission in the Americas and now serves as a local missionary sent by African and Southeast Asian archbishops! I joined an Anglican Franciscan Third Order in my continued pursuit for a life for which my heart and soul were aching. In 2006 I discovered the Brothers and Sisters of Charity. I had already held in high regard the music of John Michael Talbot, then learned he was the Founder of a Catholic community whose hermitage is in Arkansas. I discerned that much of what I sought I recognized in this community of brothers and sisters. In 2008, I made my three-year temporary profession as a domestic member of the Brothers and Sisters of Charity and I look forward to whatever God is calling me. I continue to seek a God-imaged, Christ-centered, and Spirit-filled simple life of poverty, chastity (look this one up!), and obedience with substantial silence, solitude, prayer and penance. I know that my journey is eternal and will meet its glorious destination when I pass through that door we call death and live life eternal with Christ. And until that day, with God's help, I will strive to live by the cross of our Lord Jesus Christ. *Galatians 6:14-16, "But may it never be that I would boast, except in the cross of our Lord Jesus Christ, through which the world has been crucified to me, and I to the world. For neither is circumcision anything, nor uncircumcision, but a new creation. And those who will walk by this rule, peace and mercy be upon them, and upon the Israel of God."*

I have learned that even through leading a weekly Bible study and scripture meditation group, cooking meals for the homeless, doing spiritual direction and church work, taking a class, reading, working, attending an ALS support group, writing, visiting with my parents who are still alive and active—thank you God! and playing with my grandson, I can still journal.

INTRODUCTION TO JOURNALING

To journal is to record thoughts and experiences. To journal is to keep a record of what is going on in your life, inside your soul. A diary can incorporate journaling. And journaling can also be a diary. Usually, a diary is writing down actual events, i.e., *"I got to spend time with my grandson today! He is so precious. We went to the park and just played and played. It was such a beautiful day. I will treasure this time forever!"* Keeping a diary is a way for you to look back at your life and see events. It can be very useful in helping you to remember those events you want to remember. Keeping a diary records your day to day chronological or chronos life.

Journaling records your thoughts and insights and gifts as you experience events. It records your spiritual or kairos life as it is lived in God's timing—those times when God acts in your life. Recording events in both chronos and kairos time can be quite epiphanic. Journaling reveals what is in our soul. Journaling attempts to record what is in your soul. Journaling reveals opportunities and journaling is writing within opportunities.

It is my hope that this book will reveal to you some ways to journal through every moment of your life. I've kept diaries off and on throughout my life and later learned from a very dear friend, Joann (now gone home to Jesus), that it is possible to write what is in our souls. Joann would get a sentence, a phrase, a word, an "aha" moment and write it in a notebook. I am learning to write what touches my heart and my soul at a particular moment, to write an insight or a gleaning.

As you reflect on issues, conversations, something you've read or heard or seen and then finally write what you have gleaned, you are journaling. An example of this is a poem that I've included called, "Searching." Philosophy is often a required course in a university, and in one course I took we were asked to write a paper on the search for the meaning of life. My paper was on how, if we have Christ and search for Him, we don't need to search for meaning because Christ is the meaning of life. Well, to my surprise I received an *A*. "Searching" is a summary reflection of that paper.

Journaling teaches us that even when we have answers we can look back and find that mystery and awe and questions still abound. When answers seem concrete and absolute it is time to ask different questions. The answer may still stay the same. But that's how we grow—by constantly seeking the will of God and knowing that sometimes His will for us yesterday is not His will for us today. I believe that God wants us to recognize all those aha moments in our lives. Those are the miracles!

Sometimes though there have been times when my life seemed too busy to spend time reflecting. (I can't imagine now that I've ever been too busy to reflect!) For example, I believe that when I was teaching at a women's prison my time there was devoted to showing these women the love of Christ. I would come home from a rewarding and yet sometimes very trying day and would just crash. I was mentally and spiritually exhausted. Spending time reflecting was not on my schedule, even though that was just what I needed.

The first few sections of this book share some methods of journaling. These methods are opportunities and are the kairos moments of life. As these opportunities are happening, record your thoughts and insights to help you grow spiritually.

One of the ways I journal throughout the many opportunities is by writing poetry. Hopefully, my poetry is a reflection of what was on my heart and in my soul at the time.

You will read examples of actual journalings. These are included not as the *way* to journal, but only as examples of what is possible. Come up with your own ideas. Pray and let God: Father, Son and Holy Spirit lead you in your journey through life. Life with God, the Trinity, is life in Community with God.

I've included a section of poetry that is part of the journal of my life. This section is the recording of some of the joys and sadness in my life, and several poems are just silly. The whole point is just to write. Just journal.

Life is a journey full of aha moments to our final destination—life eternal with God: Father, Son, and Holy Spirit. If I consider my life as the journey it is, I can then understand and be involved with the process. Christ saves—and we must believe and work out our salvation as the Bible teaches. *Philippians 2: 12-13, So then, my beloved, just as you have always obeyed, not as in my presence only, but now much more in my absence, work out your salvation with fear and trembling; for it is God who is at work in you, both to will and to work for His good pleasure.* Christ is both our Journey and our Destination.

The purpose of this book, dear reader, is to inspire you. It is my desire to minister to your heart as you read and reflect. It is my hope that you will be encouraged to journal through life.

Journal in prayer

Journal in worship

Journal by reflecting on:
Scripture
Work
Family
Readings
The present moment
Who the Father is
Who Christ is
Who the Holy Spirit is
Random thoughts
Words
Metaphors
+

Draw a picture:

   Of how you feel

      Of your thoughts

         Of who you want to be

            Of the child in you

               Of the Christ in you

Journal through every moment of your life.

Growth through journaling
comes from intimate time
with God: Father, Son and Holy Spirit
through prayer as
God reveals His Path
He reveals Truth
Gift
Promise
He gives Comfort
Peace
all in His time
Kairos time
Intimacy with God
will happen
any time
any place
if you are willing
to take the
chronos time
to be in
Kairos time

THE OPPORTUNITIES FOR JOURNALING

1. PRAYER

Prayer is one opportunity in which and from which we may journal. Enter prayer being open to the leading of the Holy Spirit. And then from prayer, write down what is given. This is journaling. Journal as a way to recognize when the Holy Spirit is speaking.

Simply write.

Journey

Listen

Receive

Ruminate

Offer

Change

Transform

+

Romans 12:2—And do not be conformed to this world, but be transformed by the renewing of your mind, so that you may prove what the will of God is, that which is good and acceptable and perfect.

Your Garden
Thank you God for light and love
For wind that brings new seed
And earth to plant and feed the crop
And rain to raise it up.
Then what my Lord is light and love
Without which we would die?
We cannot grow when light is not
Nor live apart from love.
Am I the seed your Spirit brought
That scatters over time?
Carry me Wind where e'er you go
Your garden waits for Thee.
Plant me Lord within your earth
To spread your precious Word
To feed your heirs so they will know
Your harvest time is near.
Quench our thirst and help us grow
Send rain that brings new life.
Your Son is here His light is sure
Your Love will raise us up!

This prayer was written over a period of years. I started it when I was sitting on an airplane headed for Portland, Oregon. It stayed unfinished for awhile. Then one day, I was reading the beginning of that journal and there it was, unfinished. Feeling the Spirit, I tweaked it a little, worked on it some more, prayed some more, and this is the result. It reflects the Great Commission given to us by Jesus just before his ascension. So, writing and journaling can and will be ongoing and unfinished. Don't be afraid to write even if it feels like it's unfinished. The Spirit will help you finish it when it's time. Write even if you think no one else will like it. God gave it to you and He likes it!

Prayers written during a *Charismatic Retreat at Home.*

Lord
What I want
And need
Should be of no
Concern of mine
You said
You would provide
Everything
I need
That suffices
You are
Sufficient

+

Accept my life
Rely on God
For healing
To be patient
With the weeds
Of my life
To realize
That Christ
Is
Sufficient
And my only
Need
To be transformed
In Christ
is my goal

+

Father, thank you
For caring about me
And loving me
I see some areas
That are dry
And
Sick
Help me
To overcome these
And be healthy in you
Please show me
What my life
Is really
Like
The good
The bad
The sick
The dry
And
To accept them
As reality
And to lean on you
For healing
Let my life
Reveal
Your marvelous healing
And work
In my life
Today
In Jesus' name
Amen

+

The following poem was written after a reflection on *Luke 15:11-32*, And He said, "A man had two sons. The younger of them said to his father, 'Father, give me the share of the estate that falls to me.' So he divided his wealth between them. And not many days later, the younger son gathered everything together and went on a journey into a distant country, and there he squandered his estate with loose living. Now when he had spent everything, a severe famine occurred in that country, and he began to be impoverished. So he went and hired himself out to one of the citizens of that country, and he sent him into his fields to feed swine. And he would have gladly filled his stomach with the pods that the swine were eating, and no one was giving anything to him. But when he came to his senses, he said, 'How many of my father's hired men have more than enough bread, but I am dying here with hunger! I will get up and go to my father, and will say to him, "Father, I have sinned against heaven, and in your sight; I am no longer worthy to be called your son; make me as one of your hired men."' So he got up and came to his father. But while he was still a long way off, his father saw him and felt compassion for him, and ran and embraced him and kissed him. And the son said to him, 'Father, I have sinned against heaven and in your sight; I am no longer worthy to be called your son.' But the father said to his slaves, 'Quickly bring out the best robe and put it on him, and put a ring on his hand and sandals on his feet; and bring the fattened calf, kill it, and let us eat and celebrate; for this son of mine was dead and has come to life again; he was lost and has been found.' And they began to celebrate. Now his older son was in the field, and when he came and approached the house, he heard music and dancing. And he summoned one of the servants and began inquiring what these things could be. And he said to him, 'Your brother has come, and your father has killed the fattened calf because he has received him back safe and sound.' But he became angry and was not willing to go in; and his father came out and began pleading with him. But he answered and said to his father, 'Look! For so many years I have been serving you and I have never neglected a command of yours; and yet you have never given me a young goat, so that I might celebrate with my friends; but when this son of yours came, who has devoured your wealth with prostitutes, you killed the fattened calf for him.' And he said to him, 'Son, you have always been with me, and all that is mine is yours. But we had to celebrate and rejoice, for this brother of yours was dead and has begun to live, and was lost and has been found.'"

Lord,
Help me to realize
When I have left God
And ask forgiveness
Then
Celebrate
With the Father
As He is celebrating
My re-turn.

Go back home
Repent
Celebrate

+

John 17:1-26, Jesus spoke these things; and lifting up His eyes to heaven, He said, "Father, the hour has come; glorify Your Son, that the Son may glorify You, even as You gave Him authority over all flesh, that to all whom You have given Him, He may give eternal life. This is eternal life, that they may know You, the only true God, and Jesus Christ whom You have sent. I glorified You on the earth, having accomplished the work which You have given Me to do. Now, Father, glorify Me together with Yourself, with the glory which I had with You before the world was. I have manifested Your name to the men whom You gave Me out of the world; they were Yours and You gave them to Me, and they have kept Your word. Now they have come to know that everything You have given Me is from You; for the words which You gave Me I have given to them; and they received them and truly understood that I came forth from You, and they believed that You sent Me. I ask on their behalf; I do not ask on behalf of the world, but of those whom You have given Me; for they are Yours; and all things that are Mine are Yours, and Yours are Mine; and I have been glorified in them. I am no longer in the world; and yet they themselves are in the world, and I come to You Holy Father, keep them in Your name, the name which You have given Me, that they may be one even as We are. While I was with them, I was keeping them in Your name which You have given Me; and I guarded them and not one of them perished but the son of perdition, so that the Scripture would be fulfilled. But now I come to You; and these things I speak in the world so that they may have My joy made full in themselves. I have given them Your word; and the world has hated them, because they are not of the world, even as I am not of the world. I do not ask You to take them out of the world, but to keep them from the evil one. They are not of the world, even as I am not of the world. Sanctify them in the truth; Your word is truth. As You sent Me into the world, I also have sent them into the world. For their sakes I sanctify Myself, that they themselves also may be sanctified in truth. I do not ask on behalf of these alone, but for those also who believe in Me through their word that they may all be one; even as You, Father, are in Me and I in You, that they also may be in Us, so that the world may believe that You sent Me. The glory which You have given Me I have given to them, that they may be one, just as We are one; I in them and You in Me, that they may be perfected in unity, so that the world may know that You sent Me, and loved them, even as You have loved Me. Father, I desire that they also, whom You have given Me, be with Me where I am, so that they may see My glory which You have given Me, for You loved Me before the foundation of the world. O righteous Father, although the world has not known You, yet I have known You; and these have known that You sent Me; and I have made Your name known to them, and will make it known, so that the love with which You loved Me may be in them, and I in them."

THOSE A-HA MOMENTS

Lord
help me to remember
your desires for me
and to also see your desires for others
so they too can be one
can be protected
can have your love
can have your joy
to be sanctified by the truth
to be in the Father
and the Son
so that Jesus
can be in them
to know your love
because of the message you bring
to be with Jesus
and see
His glory

+

Revelation 21:1-4, Then I saw a new heaven and a new earth; for the first heaven and the first earth passed away, and there is no longer any sea. And I saw the holy city, new Jerusalem, coming down out of heaven from God, made ready as a bride adorned for her husband. And I heard a loud voice from the throne, saying, "Behold, the tabernacle of God is among men, and He will dwell among them, and they shall be His people, and God Himself will be among them, and He will wipe away every tear from their eyes; and there will no longer be any death; there will no longer be any mourning, or crying, or pain; the first things have passed away."

Lord, come now
fill me
never let me go
I accept your virtues
my new life in you
and
you in me
the joy of you
and
the capacity to speak
not in words so much
but with
your
universal
language of
love

+

A Prayer is thanking God for his gifts. He creates, he gives, he sends. Friends and family come into our life as borrowed people and death is God's Gift to life eternal. This was written after my grandmother died. I was missing her, went into prayer and came out with the realization again that death is but a door to the eternal.

A PRAYER

Lord God, Heavenly Father, our Creator
You gave us Life, our beginning

Lord God, Jesus Christ, our Savior
God's Word and Love
You gave us Life eternal

Lord God, Holy Spirit, our Comforter
You are with us always.

Thank you God for creating us; for loving us; for filling us;
Thank you Father for giving us our beginning at our birth;
For giving us Life through Jesus Christ your Son, our Savior;
And for your Spirit, our Lifeline.

We wonder at Life and question at Death.
You send us family, friend, husband, wife, brother, sister,
Mother, daughter, father, son — but only for a little borrowed time.
They are not ours to keep, but only to cherish for a little while
And we thank you for that time.

LYNNETTE GOLDY

No matter how long
You've given us someone
It is always too short in our terms of time, Lord.
But your time is different.
Your time is perfect.

We pray Father, Son and Holy Spirit for your touch
Of Life and love and comfort.

We thank you our great and marvelous, wonderful,
Awesome, loving, comforting God
For Life now.

We thank you for your gift of people we have around us,
And for Life as it continues through that Gift we call Death
When we'll live Life eternal with you.
Amen

Sometimes there is a great desire to participate in God's Holy Presence. I Will...Father is a reflection of the desire to move from being the recipient of God's mercy (and yet remaining in it!) to sharing Christ with others. It was written, not to be read as one piece, but as fifteen separate petitions. Each petition can be used singularly in meditation.

I Will.....Father

Feel the warmth of Your mercy
Hear the songs of Your power
Listen to the words of Your wisdom.

Live in the cradle of Your grace
See the light of Your countenance
Immerse in the abundance of Your blessings.

Touch the splendor of Your face
Delight in the fragrance of Your holiness
Sing the psalms of Your glory.

Produce the fruits of Your vine
Share the attainment of Your peace
Pray the fulfillment of Your will.

Imitate the example of Your son
Carry the essence of Your spirit
Love your children with Your love.

This piece was written about an experience in church where we can Celebrate an Hour. The beauty of the building added to the worship experience. But church is not where our relationship, or our purpose, unfolds.

Celebrate an Hour

Cathedral ceilings and candles high
Celebrate an hour
Call on his name with jubilance
And rest in His power.

Incense burning and chanting low
Honor the Lord with praise
Entreat Adonai Almighty God
Laud Him all of your days.

Altar table and crosses call
Adore Him with your love
Supplications to your Abba
Sent through His holy dove.

Body of Christ and cleansing blood
Partake as he commands
Listen still as he comes near
Holding you in his hands.

Outside door and waiting world
His kingdom to increase
Go into the mission field
Praying for His peace.

2. REFLECTION

Another opportunity for journaling is simply reflecting on Scripture, other readings, what was shared or learned in conversations, in Bible study, at Sunday School, in church, at work and at play. Or, what comes after a seemingly non-inspirational opportunity. Sometimes the aha comes later on. You'll be doing something else, like sleeping, and all of a sudden you remember something you heard or thought and say, aha!

Examples of Reflection Journaling

I share these excerpts from my Journal to give examples of what is possible. Sometimes we think that we have nothing to say, or that God is not speaking to us. We feel we are in our dry time. But remember, God is always with us even when we don't feel Him. He is always speaking to us even when we don't hear Him. He is always near us even when we feel very far away from Him. So, write anyway. God reveals His mysteries in very mysterious ways sometimes.

> I long to rest
> in the Silence of His Words
> listening
> with the ears of my heart

My husband often says when he is ministering to others, "Stop, You Talk, I'll Listen, We'll Pray." He even has a sign that is printed with this phrase.

In this same vein, we can ask:

>God,
>Stop
>You talk
>I'll listen
>and we'll pray.
>
>God will respond
>by stopping what He's doing
>(seemingly so)
>just for us!
>He'll talk to us,
>we'll listen
>and
>prayer brings us together.
>+++

The following reflections were written after I had taken a "gifts" class and didn't feel I had any of the gifts that were revealed. I was somewhat down-in-the-dumps and after prayer and Bible reading knew that even though I may not have gifts I still had Christ.

October 29th

1 John 4:13-17, By this we know that we abide in Him and He in us, because He has given us of His Spirit. We have seen and testify that the Father has sent the Son to be the Savior of the world. Whoever confesses that Jesus is the Son of God, God abides in him, and he in God. We have come to know and have believed the love which God has for us God is love, and the one who abides in love abides in God, and God abides in him. By this, love is perfected with us, so that we may have confidence in the day of judgment; because as He is, so also are we in this world.

It is comforting to know
that whoever
lives in love
lives in God and
God in him
God is love
All said
it is comforting to know
that in spite
of a seeming lack of gifts
God still lives in us.
Amen!

+

Knowing that I belong to God
gives me joy
Even if I am good at nothing
I am joyful
because
I belong to God
Even if my only talent
is to love the Lord
that is sufficient
because
I belong to Him
He made me
and loves me
What greater gift is there
than to be loved
by Him?
These things I must remember
and write on my heart
To live for Christ
is my greatest talent

+

THOSE A-HA MOMENTS

October 31ˢᵗ

The devotional I read today was on being transformed into Christ's likeness. The Orthodox call this theosis. It's a process.

2 Corinthians 3:18, But we all, with unveiled face, beholding as in a mirror the glory of the Lord, are being transformed into the same image from glory to glory, just as from the Lord, the Spirit.

We reflect the Lord's glory
our faces reflect his glory
We are being transformed
into his likeness
with ever-increasing
glory
which comes from the Lord

+

We are all being transformed
My life is hidden
In Christ
I have a
New self
I will let the peace
Of Christ
Rule in my heart
I am called to peace
I am thankful
And whatever I do
I do in the name of my Lord and Savior
Jesus Christ

+

LYNNETTE GOLDY

Help me, Lord
To concentrate on only you
To fix
My eyes
(heart, mind, soul)
On Jesus
So that
I may become
Like
You
Into your image

+

June 8th

John 3:30, He must increase, but I must decrease.

The opposite of pride is humility and the opposite of selfishness is selflessness. I become less so others can become greater. Struggling with being right.

Do's and Don'ts to Live By

Only God has all the answers and knows all the answers
I don't and neither does anyone else
Therefore, I can quit acting like I have all the answers

1 Corinthians 2:5,…so that your faith would not rest on the wisdom of men, but on the power of God.

I will have no authoritarian answer to anything
because only God has the guaranteed answer to everything
He is the only real Authority

1 Corinthians 3:19, For the wisdom of this world is foolishness before God.

Someone else should have their way
Over my way because others are more important

Philippians 2:3, Do nothing from selfishness or empty conceit, but with humility of mind regard one another as more important than yourselves.

I will not have a preference for anything
save God Himself
and demonstrate this by honoring others

*Romans 13:10, Be devoted to one another in brotherly love;
give preference to one another in honor.*

Any questions I ask of others
I will not argue their answer
Because my trust is in God alone

*Romans 15:13, May the God of hope fill you with all joy and peace in believing,
so that you will abound in hope by the power of the Holy Spirit.*

I will let others make their points
and act as if mine are inconsequential

Luke 6:31, Treat others the same way you want them to treat you.

Others can make their comments first and last.

1 Corinthians 10:24, Let no one seek his own good, but that of his neighbor.

THOSE A-HA MOMENTS

June 30th

My spiritual director asked me to see myself from the perspective of the little girl inside of me. She asked me to draw a picture of that little girl, give her a name (Stephanie), and write down what I was like as that little girl. And to do it all with my left hand (I am right-handed). It was really fun, although I didn't see the purpose at the time. Now I realize that this helped me see the part of me that I have left behind. That little girl is still here and I need to be her more often! Have fun!

Letter from my little girl inside!

Hi I'm Stephanie. This is hard to do left-handed. I like animals — dogs, cats, lizards, grasshoppers, birds, not snakes or worms though. I like to play outside, but I can't get sunburned. I want to feel freer like I used to when I was little. I like to have an imagination. I like to pretend I am somewhere else, or someone else. I like to go on adventures. I like rocks. I hope to write stories & poetry. This is a picture of me. ← this is Eric →

sorry
my pen slipped

I want to be quiet with God. I want to play my harmonica for God — just Him & me.

6-30-03
Stephanie

Life As Journey

THOSE A-HA MOMENTS

September 14th

Wow! It's been 10 months since I've written. Have I been that busy or forgetful or preoccupied? It's been one year today that Mom broke her hip. She was a real trooper! Healed real fast—or tried to, anyway. I was reading Hebrews this morning (awake at 4:30, up at 5—had oatmeal, came back to bed to read. Max loves to come back to bed in the mornings.) Note: Max was our little dog we lost in 2009.

Hebrews 4:12-13, For the word of God is living and active and sharper than any two-edged sword, and piercing as far as the division of soul and spirit, of both joints and marrow, and able to judge the thoughts and intentions of the heart. And there is no creature hidden from His sight, but all things are open and laid bare to the eyes of Him with whom we have to do.

Some thoughts occurred to me about this. Medical science has found that sometimes our bodies adhere to, or accept, foreign objects, i.e., the shunts in my son's ear, shrapnel in soldiers' bodies. The word of God is like that—shunts and shrapnel. There to help or hinder and sometimes we accept teaching or correction and we live—go on to a better life if our bodies, we, accept that. Like the titanium hip Mom now has.

the Word of God
enters
our bodies/minds/souls
like a Sword
painful
penetrating
to separate
our sin from spirit
so we find our proper connection
with God
so spirit can be united
with the Holy Spirit of God
taking first place
in our lives

LYNNETTE GOLDY

the Sword
the Word of God
judges our thoughts
and
attitudes

the Sword remains
in our bodies
adhering to our being
becoming one
with us

constantly teaching and correcting
it is both shunt and shrapnel

if we reject the Sword
as a body may reject the shunt,
we try again
another sword
another shunt
until we accept it
until the Sword
penetrates and becomes one
with us
finally

if we reject the Sword
as a body may reject the shrapnel
as a poison
we then die—
never to accept
the Sword
the Word of God

January 15th

Romans 2:28-29, For he is not a Jew who is one outwardly, nor is circumcision that which is outward in the flesh. But he is a Jew who is one inwardly; and circumcision is that which is of the heart, by the Spirit, not by the letter; and his praise is not from men, but from God.

Circumcised heart = think about the real, medical circumcision. Skin is cut off of the outside. A circumcised heart is a heart in which an outer thing (layer) has been cut off to reveal what is underneath, inside. Painful, but beneficial. If praise is not from men, but from God; then so should condemnation be not from men.

Lord
help me to not look
at what
someone
eats, or drinks, or wears
To not even be concerned—
that is one's own journey
What is important
is underneath
inside
the person

June 24th

Reflections from the book, "Community and Growth" by Jean Vanier.

What is important is
Unity
Not division
Love
Not hate

Find what is
Sameness
Not difference
Peace
Not chaos
Communion
Not individualism
Community
Not individuality

Remain in Community
With Father, Son, and Holy Spirit
In the Presence of God
Gift and grace
In the Present moment
Wait upon the Lord

June 29th

I participated in a three-day *Charismatic Retreat at Home*. These are some of my reflections from that time spent at a cabin in the mountains of Colorado.

Luke 8:5-15, "The sower went out to sow his seed; and as he sowed, some fell beside the road, and it was trampled under foot and the birds of the air ate it up. Other seed fell on rocky soil, and as soon as it grew up, it withered away, because it had no moisture. Other seed fell among the thorns; and the thorns grew up with it and choked it out. Other seed fell into the good soil, and grew up, and produced a crop a hundred times as great. As He said these things, He would call out, 'He who has ears to hear, let him hear.'" His disciples began questioning Him as to what this parable meant. And He said, "To you it has been granted to know the mysteries of the kingdom of God, but to the rest it is in parables, so that seeing they may not see, and hearing they may not understand. Now the parable is this: the seed is the word of God. Those beside the road are those who have heard; then the devil comes and takes away the word from their heart, so that they will not believe and be saved. Those on the rocky soil are those who, when they hear, receive the word with joy; and these have no firm root; they believe for a while, and in time of temptation fall away. The seed which fell among the thorns, these are the ones who have heard, and as they go on their way they are choked with worries and riches and pleasures of this life, and bring no fruit to maturity. But the seed in the good soil, these are the ones who have heard the word in an honest and good heart, and hold it fast, and bear fruit with perseverance."

Am I the planter?
Where do I plant the Word?
Am I not careful and
Scatter them on the path
On rocks
In thorns
Not caring that they won't grow?
Am I wasting
The Word of God?
Should I be more careful
Where I plant?

\+

What kind of soil am I?
Hard, dry, non-absorbent?
Fertile, soft, retain and produce?

\+

Listen to God
Accept Him
Let his rain of love be absorbed
into my being
the dirt
the ground
Let others be the nourishment
to prepare
my being
my dirt
to produce
The Kingdom within

\+

Patience
the weeds
others
worry
God will weed them out
The Word will weed them out
Patience
let God work
in me

THOSE A-HA MOMENTS

2 Chronicles 7:11-16, Thus Solomon finished the house of the LORD and the king's palace, and successfully completed all that he had planned on doing in the house of the LORD and in his palace. Then the LORD appeared to Solomon at night and said to him, "I have heard your prayer and have chosen this place for Myself as a house of sacrifice. If I shut up the heavens so that there is no rain, or if I command the locust to devour the land, or if I send pestilence among My people, and My people who are called by My name humble themselves and pray and seek My face and turn from their wicked ways, then I will hear from heaven, will forgive their sin and will heal their land. Now My eyes will be open and My ears attentive to the prayer offered in this place. For now I have chosen and consecrated this house that My name may be there forever, and My eyes and My heart will be there perpetually."

Testing

Sometimes I think the rain
Has stopped in my life
The rain that waters
The dry arid ground
Of my life
Could Eric's illness
Be the locusts
That have come to devour
Not just his life
But mine as well?
We are one life
Not two
So what devours him
Devours me as well
If I ignore it
It is there
If I run from it
It is there
If I hide
It is there

There is no escape.
Lord, I know this is
Not punishment
Because your blood,
Your ultimate sacrifice
Your love
Covers over everything
It doesn't feel
Like love.
Your love
Is hard to comprehend
To understand.
Your love is mystery
But you are love
You are mystery
Which is where
Faith comes in
Lord, you had faith
In your disciples
You prayed for them
You prayed for the world
To your Father in heaven
You gave your life
Into your Father's hands.
Lord Christ
Have faith in us
Pray for us
We give our lives
Into your hands.

+

Emergence

God has chosen us
As his temple
He will be
Attentive
To the prayers
Offered
In this place
In us
He chose
And
Consecrated
Us
So that his name
May be here
Forever
In us
Forever
His eyes and heart
Will
Be
With us
Forever

+

The following are two excerpts written during a Brothers and Sisters of Charity annual gathering of domestic members at Little Portion Hermitage in Berryville, Arkansas.

(Note: On Tuesday, April 29, 2008, a fire destroyed the building and much of the beautiful gardens described below. I am blessed to have spent time here before the fire consumed what moth and rust would have eventually destroyed. The people enveloped in Christ with the Holy Spirit are the real beauty.)

October 3rd

The Hermitage is beautiful! Gardens and flowers and herbs. There's a building with a porch around it. Below the back porch is a walkway in the garden beautifully landscaped. Part of it is covered with wood slats and that is covered with a green vine. There's a lily pond in this garden with lily pads. The rock and stone walkways are hand-laid and beautiful. The people here are much loved and loving. I was greeted with, "Welcome Home." I felt I truly had come home.

October 7th

So what have I learned at the gathering?
To praise God at all times
To speak thoughtfully
And slowly
To do prayer slowly
And prayerfully
To be vulnerable
To learn
Recognize
Use my gifts
To be more humble
To study humility
To love all
To be helpful
To obey

+

October 11th

1 Peter 3:8-12, To sum up, all of you be harmonious, sympathetic, brotherly, kindhearted, and humble in spirit; not returning evil for evil or insult for insult, but giving a blessing instead; for you were called for the very purpose that you might inherit a blessing. For, the one who desires life, to love and see good days, must keep his tongue from evil and his lips from speaking deceit. He must turn away from evil and do good; he must seek peace and pursue it. For the eyes of the Lord are toward the righteous, and his ears attend to their prayer, but the face of the Lord is against those who do evil.

This scripture says to return a blessing instead of evil for evil or insult for insult.

Be kind
like-minded
sympathetic
loving and humble
We are called to all this
and to give blessings
and to return blessings
Help me to do this, Father
to really watch what comes out of my mouth
Help me also to watch what goes into my mouth
To be healthy inside
and outside
To be God's temple inside
and outside
that everything I say
be an outward example of an inward grace
May what I say
and do
reflect what I feel
and who I am
And may I feel and be

LYNNETTE GOLDY

a child of God
to be God's
temple

\+

GI-GO
garbage in — garbage out
BI-BO
blessings in — blessings out
PI-PO
praise in-praise out
peace in-peace out
Seek Peace!

\+

THOSE A-HA MOMENTS

On February 13th, after praying for my sister on her birthday, I decided to give her some starter jars of seeds for her to sprout. Considering the process it takes for seeds to sprout, it occurred to me that Christ undertook a similar process and that we as Christians accept that same process for ourselves.

Happy Birthday! These jars of quinoa and lentils will soon become sprouts! Pay attention to what is involved and you will see that we are not unlike these precious seeds.

Directions

Immerse them in the waters of baptism
(soak seeds in water for 12 to 24 hours)

Lift them out of the water
(drain the water and set jar at 45 degree angle for 12 hours)

Pour God's love over them for three days
(rinse and drain & set at 45 degree angle for 12 hours over a period of three days)

When we produce fruits of the Spirit
(watch the sprouts grow!)

Then others will enjoy the Christ in us!
(refrigerate just as they are and enjoy!)

Sunday School, May 31ˢᵗ

An example of God's righteous indignation from *Hosea 13:8, I will encounter them like a bear robbed of her cubs, And I will tear open their chests; There I will also devour them like a lioness, As a wild beast would tear them.*

Jesus had righteous indignation when he was in the temple and turned over the moneychangers' table. Jesus was God and man. He did not have man's anger, but God's righteous indignation! I cannot presume to ever have righteous indignation or to label my anger, at any time, righteous indignation because there is a greater chance of blasphemy, of sinning in my anger, than the chance that my anger is indeed authentic righteous indignation. Can people possess the righteous indignation that belongs to God? And why would I want to take that chance that mine is righteous? I wouldn't. That would be very prideful, hubris. And pride goes before the fall. And if I insist on my humility, then I would be prideful. I will leave that determination to God. If causal change is the goal of possessing righteous indignation, I would rather be the instrument through contemplative prayer which leads to transformation.

I want to be raised up!
Oh, Jesus, raise me up!
I'm not wise enough
to know the difference
between
humanity's righteous indignation and anger
They both look like madness

+

THOSE A-HA MOMENTS

June 23rd

How we eat and sleep
and walk and talk
and pray and work and play
all come from inside of us
The kind of life I lead or desire
spills into all of life
If I desire the contemplative life
then when I eat I practice mindfulness
I remember where our food comes from
I remember how it was raised or grown
cultivated
nourished
produced
harvested
transported
Mindful eating
is to give honor to the food
we eat
It is to give thanks to God
for this food having lived
and having given up its life
to nourish me
Through mindfulness
and fasting
I can learn that I do not exist
outside of everything else
Through Christ
all His creation is connected
If I desire to sleep well
I must live well
If I desire to live well
I must be aware of everything
and everyone

around me
I do not exist alone
If I desire to walk and talk
and pray and work
and play nice with others
I must remember
that all is community
I must remember
that the Father, Son and Holy Spirit
do not exist alone
I must remember
that God is Community-in-One
and that living within that
is to live life
intentionally
mindful
of Community
+

In the Beginning, God is a story of God the Trinity's gift to us of the tree and how a simple tree can mean so much. It was written after a Bible study when a connection between the first tree of life and the crucifixion tree was realized.

IN THE BEGINNING, GOD

In the beginning, God.
And God created.
He created many wonderful things,
Too precious and too awesome for us to behold.
However, God gave us dominion
Over all His creation.
He said to us, Subdue —
Replenish —
Dress, till and keep My Earth.
But of one tree you cannot touch.

In the beginning, God.
The Father sent His only Son.
He named Him Jesus, the Christ,
Too precious and too awesome for us to behold.
However, God gave His Son to us
His best creation.
He said to Him, Heal—
Perform miracles—
Change water into wine.
And of one tree Christ knew He'd carry.

In the beginning, God.
The Father knew His Son would die.
His Only Son would die for the sins
of His best creation.
He told us the earth was ours
But one tree we could not touch.

He told us that Christ was ours
and one tree He'd have to touch.
The Son lived and taught and loved.
He healed and performed miracles,
And on one tree, He suffered.

In the beginning, God.
The Father knew His Son had died.
He was denied, betrayed and whipped.
We nailed Him down.
His sweat was blood, He suffered so.
He cried to His Father, He was so alone.
He was naked and we gambled His cloak.
He was thirsty and we gave Him vinegar.
We had subdued,
He had healed.
Now, from one tree, we're alone.

In the beginning, God
And God's Son died.
The temple curtain tore in two,
The earth shook and rocks split,
The dead were alive again.
Jesus rose and walked with us.
He showed us His hands and feet,
He ate with us.
Jesus ascended. He lifted His hands,
blessed us
and was taken into heaven.

In the beginning, God.
The Father received His Only Son
But He loved us too much to leave us alone.
So He sent His Spirit to watch,
To comfort,

THOSE A-HA MOMENTS

To heal and renew;
From the Garden and one untouchable tree
to Golgotha and one suffering tree,
From the Beginning and Creation
to Eternity and Salvation.

As a child, did you ever think your parents looked alike? In His Image will describe what happens when we have a personal relationship with Christ.

In His Image

Our relationship with Christ
Is like a marriage.

It's real intense at first.
Everything is magnified.
Flowers are vibrant.
Sunsets are more brilliant.
He's irresistible in every way. You can hardly wait to see him.
You find that you miss him terribly when you're away.
You want to brag about him to others.
You find new things about him all the time.
You begin to know
What to expect of him,
And you are learning
What he expects of you.
Soon, there is a level of
Comfort about the
Relationship.
He can still surprise you,
And you may not
Brag about him as often.

But you begin to look like him.

THOSE A-HA MOMENTS

Island Far Away is a description of a dream, but yet is also a description of another reality. As soon as I woke up one morning, I wrote this down. There is great symbolism in this piece. In fact, I'm still seeing symbolism many years later as my understanding progresses.

Island Far Away

Some day I'll move to an island
an island far away
Become one with the local folks
and live and work and play.

I'll set up house on that island
so warm and misty there
And live amidst the village huts
to breathe the clean fresh air.

Streets are narrow and teach us much
with sand between our toes
There trees reach out and give us shade
and veil the bright sun's glows.

The rain will come the rain will go
to wash our bodies bare
Then just as quickly hide again
as if it didn't care.

Bring coconuts and basket reed
to sell in market fair
The fruits of our labor gleaned
are all we have to share

LYNNETTE GOLDY

Life on this island is fairer
in dreams than when awake
I hear the ocean waves lapping
oh sleep let me partake.

When one must die it is to live
death's not our final page
The clay cools our visible shells
on this small island stage.

Some day I'll move to an island
an island far away
Become one with the local folks
where life shall live the play.

THOSE A-HA MOMENTS

My Walk Above the Clay is similar to Island Far Away in meaning. This time, however, it is the journey that is important rather than the actual place. The journey in this case is one of deep Christian meditation and being in the Presence of God.

My Walk Above the Clay

The flowers sang out to me brightly
along the pathway that led away.
All around me their warmth was lively
and my walk rose above the clay.

Their sweet smelling fragrance gave license
to follow after the day.
The stars absorbed their silence
and, in turn, reflected the way.

The view ahead grew lighter
and I longed for what there did lay.
The world beyond was much brighter
in the garden along the pathway.

My heartbeats increased unceasingly
as I heard the sun's voice in its ray.
I turned and saw how familiarly
towards home our tears marked the way.

The flowers sang out to me brightly
along the pathway that led away.
All around me their warmth was lively
as my walk returned to the clay.

Searching is based on the title of a college term paper called "The Search for Meaning" that was submitted years ago to a professor in a philosophy class. We were told to write a paper on the search for the meaning of life. (I got an A.) This piece is based on John 3:16 and describes that paper's content.

Searching

the search for meaning
title of a college class
philosophy, theology, opinion

For God So Loved the World

the design of a cause
be precise in every reason
rationale, motive, occasion

That He Gave His Only Begotten Son

the methods of a search
choose the manner carefully
process, technique, fashion

That Whoever Believes in Him

the meaning of meaning
and which interpretation
persuasion, religion, postulation

Shall Not Perish

the search for meaning
the design of a cause

THOSE A-HA MOMENTS

the methods of a search
the meaning of meaning

But Have Eternal Life

+

At one point I wanted to remember all the different stages I had gone through. After writing them down I put them in the form of a cross to remind myself that without God my life is meaningless. Five words are repeated within. These five words represent what seems to be my life in the most general sense. Without these five elements I would dry up and blow away.

```
                    stages

                     life
                   daughter
                 sister friend
                love hate laugh
                    student
                   fun trust
                    cousin
                     niece
            granddaughter greatniece
                    shame
                     cry
                     love
                    learn
                   try laugh
              sister-in-law aunt
                 wife mother
                daughter-in-law
                 mother-in-law
                   mistake
                     cry
                    learn
                    laugh
             hugs intimate boundary
                    health
                    death
```

THOSE A-HA MOMENTS

cry
love
laugh
life

The Road that Leads From Here is about the straight and narrow road and recovery from anything that separates you from God. Even I was surprised when I wrote the last stanza.

The Road That Leads From Here

The road that leads from here
is a straight road
but where does it go
I don't know.
it's a narrow road
one at a time
please.

The road that leads from here
is a flowering road
and scented so sweet
what a treat.
it's a burgeoning road
line up now your
turn.

The road that leads from here
is all one way
and no detours
follow the rules.
it's a happy road
are you ready to
go?

The road that leads from here
is different still
than what you
understood.

THOSE A-HA MOMENTS

it's an everlasting road
can't take baggage
though.

This is a reflection after reading the following verses:

Hosea 13:15, Though he flourishes among the reeds, An east wind will come, The wind of the LORD coming up from the wilderness; And his fountain will become dry And his spring will be dried up; It will plunder his treasury of every precious article.

Exodus 33:21-23, Then the LORD said, "Behold, there is a place by Me, and you shall stand there on the rock; and it will come about, while My glory is passing by, that I will put you in the cleft of the rock and cover you with My hand until I have passed by. Then I will take My hand away and you shall see My back, but My face shall not be seen."

Exodus 17:6, "Behold, I will stand before you there on the rock at Horeb; and you shall strike the rock, and water will come out of it, that the people may drink." And Moses did so in the sight of the elders of Israel.

1 Corinthians 2:6-8, Yet we do speak wisdom among those who are mature; a wisdom, however, not of this age nor of the rulers of this age, who are passing away; but we speak God's wisdom in a mystery, the hidden wisdom which God predestined before the ages to our glory; the wisdom which none of the rulers of this age has understood; for if they had understood it they would not have crucified the Lord of glory.

.

The East Wind
A Dry Flood
Dries the floods of my life
You are the Desert of Life

What can quench my thirst
But the Waters of Life
From the Rock of Life
In the Desert of Life

Christ is the Rock
Lord, hide me
in the cleft
of Your
Rock

THOSE A-HA MOMENTS

You are the
Water
That came out
Of the Rock
The Water of Life

Lord let me drink
Of the Everlasting
Water

Quench my thirsty dry life
Let your Waters roll
Over me as I am
Hidden
In the cleft of Your Rock

As the Wind Dries my life
Your Water Gives me Life
So that Your Life
Is what Lives in me
And I in You

+

3. CHRISTIAN MEDITATION

My favorite opportunity for journaling comes though Christian meditation.

Christian meditation can be an integral element in journaling. Christian meditation is prayer with our God: Father, Son, and Holy Spirit. Nothing is more precious than sitting with the one we love and who loves us, God.

> Being in the presence of someone
> completely present
> giving that person your full attention
> listening only to them
> is the highest form of respect and love

Before beginning to meditate on scripture or on Christ or the Holy Spirit, ask God to be present to you through His Spirit. Sit quietly. There is not a secret way to sit. There is not a succinct prescription for this method of prayer. Simply begin with prayer and then read a verse or two of Scripture, such as *Psalm 46:10, Be Still, and know that I am God* (KJV). Repeating scripture prayerfully sets the tone. After all, you are listening to God's word. Ask yourself, what is this scripture saying to me? What is God saying to me through this particular scripture? Is it telling you to be quiet and listen? Perhaps it tells you that God is indeed our great God and creator. And how can we know this? By further reading and studying and praying and developing a relationship with Christ. Recall or read other scripture. Listen to what you read. After a few moments, write down what came to you through your reading and listening, through your attention to Christ. What has the Holy Spirit revealed to you during this time of listening and reading His word? Listen with the ears of your heart and write what you hear. This is similar to lectio divina, but much simpler.

Another form of Christian meditation is to read a story or parable from the Bible. Picture yourself within this story. Be in this story with Christ, and with the other participants in this story. What are they saying? What is happening? Imagine the setting. What is the temperature? Is it warm or cold? Is it raining? Is it day or night? What are you thinking as the story takes place? Is there an emotion you are feeling as you are in this story? Are you standing in a field or on the road? What can you smell? When you have imagined and felt all that can be imagined and felt during this time with this scripture, write down what you have learned and experienced.

Some other things you can meditate on might be a cross, or a picture of Christ. Thinking about what Christ has done for you by dying for you can be very healing. Thinking about who Christ is as the Son of God, as the Savior of the world can be very therapeutic—after all, He is the Great Physician! What thoughts come to mind, what emotions come when you meditate on these things? Write them down.

These methods take practice. Have fun with these methods of prayer. God is not boring. He wants you to have fun and enjoy being with Him. Be grateful for this time. Thank God for His love and tell Him you look forward to spending some more precious time with Him soon.

Practice
Presence
Listen
Attentive
Re-turn
Be
Journal

Proverbs 3:3
Let not mercy and truth forsake thee:
bind them about thy neck;
write them upon the tablet of thine heart.
(KJV)

Suggested Scripture for Christian Meditation

Job 22:21a   Yield now and be at peace with Him

Psalm 4:8   In peace I will both lie down and sleep, For You alone, O LORD, make me to dwell in safety.

Psalm 5:3   In the morning, O LORD, You will hear my voice; In the morning I will order my prayer to You and eagerly watch.

Psalm 25:21   Let integrity and uprightness preserve me; for I wait for you.

Psalm 27:14   Wait for the LORD; Be strong and let your heart take courage; Yes, wait for the LORD.

Psalm 33:20   Our soul waits for the LORD: he is our help and our shield.

Psalm 37:7a   Rest in the LORD and wait patiently for Him;

Psalm 39:7   *And now, Lord, for what do I wait? My hope is in You.*

Psalm 46:10a Be still, and know that I am God. (KJV)

Psalm 130:5   I wait for the LORD, my soul does wait, And in His word do I hope.

Proverbs 14:30a   A tranquil heart is life to the body.

Isaiah 14:7a   The whole earth is at rest and is quiet.

Isaiah 32:18   And my people shall dwell…in quiet resting places. (KJV)

Isaiah 54:10   For the mountains may be removed and the hills may shake, But My loving kindness will not be removed from you, And My covenant of peace will not be shaken, says the LORD who has compassion on you.

Mark 4:39   …Peace, be still…(KJV)

John 14:27   Peace I leave with you; My peace I give to you; not as the world gives do I give to you. Do not let your heart be troubled, nor let it be fearful.

1 Thessalonians 4:11a   Make it your ambition to lead a quiet life.

1 Timothy 2:2b   That we may lead a quiet and peaceable life in all godliness and honesty. (KJV)

1 Peter 3:4   but let it be the hidden person of the heart, with the imperishable quality of a gentle and quiet spirit, which is precious in the sight of God.

Before you begin Christian meditation or begin any reading, ask the Holy Spirit to be present with you. Focus on God. Pray to be God-imaged, Christ-centered, and Spirit-filled. Keep the eyes of your heart on Jesus. Be open to whatever God has for you. Listen to what God is saying to you. Don't do all the talking in prayer. Listen. If you do all the talking, then when do you listen?

So, right now take a few minutes. Go to a quiet place. Ask God to be with you as you re-turn to the Lord. Then repeat a chosen scripture slowly and attentively. Meditate on the scripture or some other reading or story or the cross. When finished, pray the prayer Jesus taught His disciples.

Now, write down the thoughts that came to you. Write down a prayer that may have been given you.

You, my friend, have just journaled.

Silent Breath was written during meditation and prayer when a great need for silence amidst a noisy life was felt.

Silent Breath

Lord, take me to the Quiet
The Silence that I hear
Breathing within me
Hurry or there will be no me left
My soul remains entrapped
Within the noise
And no one hears my cry

Christ In Me was written after a time of prayer when I awoke at 2:30 a.m. I usually can go back to sleep but decided to get up and do some Bible reading. Perhaps this was the dark night of my soul, followed by my rebirth. Towards the end of my writing, I was so overcome by God's forgiveness that I wept. I knew that the Holy Spirit was in me, around me, through me, and had enclosed me.

Christ In Me

The only way for Christ to live in me
is for me to die. Die to self and live to Christ.
Die to self? OR Self must die.
Live to Christ OR Christ must live.
But I don't kill my self.
Self will just shrivel up
and die on its own because there will be no room
for self when Christ grows and lives in me.
I must not concentrate on self dying.
I cannot seek for self to die.
My goal is not to die to self.
My goal is not that self must die.
I must seek Christ.
My goal must be Christ.
My goal is that Christ must live.
Do not murder. Even do not murder self.
I feel that Christ is growing and living in me.
I feel that self is dying. I must mourn self.
I will grieve my dying. For a time.
And at the same time I rejoice and celebrate the birth of
Christ in me—
I am a new creation.
2 Corinthians 12:9
2 Corinthians 5:17
Am I in Christ or is Christ in me?

Colossians 1:27!
Philippians 1:21
Life is Christ!
Christ in me and I in Christ.
Must be both.

John 14:6
I am the way, and the truth, and the life.
No one comes to the Father unless by me.
Christ is Life.
Christ is the living water.
Jeremiah 17:7-8
I am the tree whose roots grow to His stream and are fed by His water.
The water of Life.
I must be fed by nothing except Christ who is Life.
Life comes from nothing except Christ.
Christ is Life.
Christ is Life in me, and I am in Christ.
Jesus prayed that his disciples would be one just as He and His Father are One.
Food may keep my body alive
but Christ keeps my soul alive.
It is better to die now and live forever
than to live now and die forever.
But self must die forever, not the Christ in me.
The Christ in me must and will live forever.
The Christ in me can never die but
He will not live in me unless I die and let Him live.
Christ died once so I can live forever.
Now, I must die so Christ can live forever in me.
But my death will be over and over and over again
every day.
My death will be a continual sacrifice so that Christ will live in me forever.

But what kind of a sacrifice is it for me to die?
for my self to die?
For my self to die is nothing compared to Jesus' dying.

Jesus died so that I can live!
Jesus died so that He can live in me!
My self is dying
so I can live in Christ.
Christ has already died so that
I can live.
Now I must die so Christ can live.
But my sacrifice is nothing compared to the sacrifice Jesus gave.
Christ will live even if I do not die, but
He will not live in me if I do not die.
I desire to die.
I desire that Christ lives in me.
Through baptism, I died and Christ began
to live in me.
But I didn't let Him live.
I kept crucifying Him
over and over again.
I wanted to live—I enjoyed my sin.
With every sin I put another nail
into His hands,
into His feet,
into His heart.
I didn't consciously do this, but
sin made me blind to my own actions.
Please forgive me Father,
forgive me Christ,
forgive me Holy Spirit.
as I look into your eyes on that cross
I see your forgiveness,
but I am unworthy of your forgiveness.

THOSE A-HA MOMENTS

What?
You made the cross?
You knew
I would hammer the nails into your hands
so you couldn't hold me?
You knew
I would hammer the nails into your feet
so you couldn't walk with me?
But I didn't hammer a nail into your heart?
Then I just thought I did?
It felt like I put a nail through your heart.

Oh,
it was *my* heart in which I hammered that nail.
I am so sorry.

And yet,
because you are LOVE,
because you are LIFE,
you have forgiven me.
Now, it is not my heart that lives in me:
It is your heart,
your love,
your life
that lives in me.
Lord Christ, you are risen in me.
Hallelujah!
You are risen indeed.

Born Again is a reflection written during one of my morning prayer and meditation times. This is a very personal description of what happened a few days earlier.

Born Again

The process of my being reborn
began with pregnancy.
For a time, I prepared for my rebirth.
I could feel the love of Christ welling up inside of me.
I could feel it kicking and grabbing onto my ribs
with such force
that it was painful.
I wanted to get beyond the preparation
and I longed to see the birth of Christ
within me.
Finally, the day came and it was a huge surprise.
My sin was revealed through the labor
and it too was painful.
I almost wanted to change my mind
and stop the birth.
In order for me to be born again,
I had to die
and part of me didn't want to die.
But I looked forward to what was
emerging.
I struggled through the pain and finally that one breath,
the Holy Spirit,
was released
and Christ was born within me.
I wept as I felt His forgiveness.
I laughed and I danced
(if only in my soul).
I rejoiced.

THOSE A-HA MOMENTS

But it was not over.
Something else was being born.
I released my former self
and I died.
I released all the sin that I held dear.
Christ held it,
examined it
to make sure it was whole,
that nothing was left inside,
and then
He discarded it.
I felt the love of Christ,
I held Christ who was born within me.
But this is still not the end.
Christ within me will grow,
if nourished,
if loved
and
if protected.
And with Him
through the Holy Spirit
and the grace of God my Father,
I will live forever

4. LECTIO DIVINA

Lectio divina is a type of prayer. One goal of lectio divina is that practicing this method of prayer will lead you to rest in the Presence of God by praying the Scriptures. Another goal is that your life will indeed be God-imaged, Christ-centered, and Spirit-filled.

The Four Parts to Lectio are:

Reading & Listening
Meditation
Prayer
Contemplation

Lectio Divina is very ancient. It is a method being kept alive in the Christian monastic tradition. One reads Scripture slowly, deliberately, and prayerfully, contemplating each Word. The Scriptures, the Word of God, then become a means of union with God. For we were created in the image and likeness of God and Christ is in us just as He is in the Father and the Father is in Him.

Lectio: Reading and Listening

We begin lectio divina by listening with the ears of our hearts, honing the gift of listening deeply to God. Remember how the prophet Elijah listened for the still small voice of God in I Kings 19:11-13? *So He said, "Go forth and stand on the mountain before the LORD." And behold, the LORD was passing by! And a great and strong wind was rending the mountains and breaking in pieces the rocks before the LORD; but the LORD was not in the wind.*

And after the wind an earthquake, but the LORD was not in the earthquake. After the earthquake a fire, but the LORD was not in the fire; and after the fire a sound of a gentle blowing. When Elijah heard it, he wrapped his face in his mantle and went out and stood in the entrance of the cave and behold, a voice came to him and said, "What are you doing here, Elijah?" Listen gently to the Presence of God through His Word, the Scriptures. The voice of God often speaks very quietly so we must learn to listen attentively. We must be silent and wait. In lectio divina we must first be still and quiet and listen to God's Word to us, given to us in this moment.

Meditatio: Meditation

When we listen to God speaking to us through His Word, the Scriptures, we ruminate on it. Picture an animal chewing its cud quietly and slowly. This is an ancient metaphor used as a symbol of Christians pondering the Word of God. We take that Word and gently repeat it silently, allowing it to cover over all of our thoughts, hopes, pain, desires and joys. This is meditating on the Word of God. We allow His Word to become His Word for us. His Word can and will touch us deeply. When we listen to the Word of God, we not only hear Him, but we actively pay attention. How do we allow His Word to become His Word for us? How do we "pay" our attention to God? By taking what we have heard and learned from Him out into the world which is the mission field.

Oratio: Prayer

Next is prayer. Prayer is communication, a conversation, being in His Presence, just being with Him and listening, and offering all of our self to Him, offering even the parts we never thought He would want. But he wants all of us, even the ugly parts. We allow the Word we have taken in to touch and transform us. Be ye, therefore, transformed by the renewing of your minds.

Contemplatio: Contemplation

Lastly we rest in the Presence of God. Be attentive to only God. Just being with Him means so much! Just as we are content to just be with someone we love. And how much do we love our Lord!

> Words are unnecessary
> because what is important
> is the time we spend together

Just experience God. Nothing need be said. Just the comfort of His Presence is enough. Here also are we silent. Just enjoy being in His Presence. From this contemplation in prayer can grow contemplation in life.

+++++++

Putting Lectio Divina Into Practice:

Choose a passage of Scripture, from one verse to several.

Read the passage slowly, reverently, proclaim the Word.

Read the passage again, slowly, ever so slowly, listening with the ear of your heart.

Choose a word or phrase from the reading that speaks to you and inwardly digest it.

Offer to God your self, your pain, your concerns, your joys and gently recite over them the word or phrase, allowing your self to be touched and transformed by the Word.

Now simply rest in the Presence of God who has used His Word to invite you to accept His transforming embrace. *Be still, and know that I Am God* (Psalm 46:10, KJV).

Journal what you have learned, be it a word or phrase, a feeling or thought. How will you let this help you grow as a Christian? Will you recognize the aha moments when they present themselves?

Here are some examples of my reflections from meditations during lectio divina:

Revelation 21:3-4, I heard a loud voice from the throne saying, "Behold, God's dwelling is with the human race. He will dwell with them and they will be his people and God himself will always be with them (as their God). He will wipe every tear from their eyes, and there shall be no more death or mourning, wailing or pain, (for) the old order has passed away."

The Holy Spirit
is telling me
that we can have this now
we have Christ now
we have Christ within us
we are new creations
born anew
so even now
the old has passed away

1 John 4:15-18, Whoever acknowledges that Jesus is the Son of God, God remains in him and he in God. We have come to know and to believe in the love God has for us. God is love, and whoever remains in love remains in God and God in him. In this is love brought to perfection among us, that we have confidence on the day of judgment because as he is, so are we in this world. There is no fear in love, but perfect love drives out fear because fear has to do with punishment, and so one who fears is not yet perfect in love.

God is in me
and I have felt His love
Jesus is love
brought to perfection
among us
We are Christ with skin on
herein
is our love made perfect
(among us)
Jesus!

THOSE A-HA MOMENTS

Matthew 13:16-17, But blessed are your eyes, because they see, and your ears, because they hear. Amen, I say to you, many prophets and righteous people longed to see what you see but did not see it, and to hear what you hear but did not hear it.

Such a feeling of the Spirit
I have tonight!
Prophets and righteous people
long to see
— I long to see, too!
What Jesus sees!
This Scripture says
we can and we do see what He sees
Scripture is living
and
active Word of God
—living and active
thoughts of God
Grow in grace
and the knowledge

What will I do to help me grow? I'm going to read Scripture every day, pray, center—long to see Jesus. Think before I speak. Be more apophatic.

Mark 4:21-25, He said to them, "Is a lamp brought in to be placed under a bushel basket or under a bed, and not to be placed on a lampstand? For there is nothing hidden except to be made visible; nothing is secret except to come to light. Anyone who has ears to hear ought to hear." He also told them, "Take care what you hear. The measure with which you measure will be measured out to you, and still more will be given to you. To the one who has, more will be given; from the one who has not, even what he has will be taken away."

Like yeast—the measure with which you measure will be measured out to you, and still more will be given to you, like *Gal. 5:9, A little leaven leavens the whole lump of dough.* Does a light speak? How does a light make hidden things visible? Is it by speaking to someone about Christ or is it letting them see the light you have? How is my life a light to others? Christ is the light or lamp, I am the lampstand which holds the light. One light in a world of darkness throws out a lot of light. Do people see the light of Christ in me?

After reading *Psalm 27:7-9, Hear, O LORD, when I cry with my voice, And be gracious to me and answer me. When You said, "Seek My face," my heart said to You, "Your face, O LORD, I shall seek." Do not hide Your face from me, Do not turn Your servant away in anger; You have been my help; Do not abandon me nor forsake me, O God of my salvation!*

Seek and come seek. Go to God, don't wait for Him to come to me. God is the I AM. He is. He is not I Do. Expecting a miracle is great, but don't expect Him to perform miracles as if that's all we want out of God, but have a relationship with Him!

After reading *Isaiah 41:10, Do not fear, for I am with you; Do not anxiously look about you, for I am your God. I will strengthen you, surely I will help you, Surely I will uphold you with My righteous right hand.*

I need to totally rely on God. Turn my stuff over to God, as well as other people's stuff that I worry about. I am with you! He says. God sees me as I am. I don't see me as I am. The more I see me as I am then

I can better relate to God and only through his grace. Surrender, trust in Him! We can't be filled until we're empty. Faith is being willing to empty ourselves so God can fill us with Himself. We are God's word-pictures.

Some more excerpts from my lectio divina journal:

Go to God, don't wait for Him to come to me.

Die to self, live in Christ.

Come to know—it's a journey.

God can't fill us until we're empty.

Love only God and loving others will follow naturally.

Titus 1:15-16, To the pure, all things are pure; but to those who are defiled and unbelieving, nothing is pure, but both their mind and their conscience are defiled. They profess to know God, but by their deeds they deny Him, being detestable and disobedient and worthless for any good deed.

When we have Christ, we are pure or clean and we see Christ in others: even the "unfit" and disobedient are pure and clean to us and to Christ. If we have Christ within us, then we see all others as Christ, as pure and clean.

Control is the great pretender. We need to die to self.

2 Tim 4:1b-5, I solemnly charge you in the presence of God and of Christ Jesus, who is to judge the living and the dead, and by His appearing and His kingdom: Preach the word; be ready in season and out of season reprove, rebuke, exhort, with great patience and instruction. For the time will come when they will not endure sound doctrine; but wanting to have their ears tickled, they will accumulate for themselves teachers in accordance to their own desires, and will turn away their ears from the truth and will turn aside to myths. But you, be sober in all things, endure hardship, do the work of an evangelist, fulfill your ministry.

The time will come and now is when people will turn to other things, not the Word, Truth. I can only change me and what I do, say, believe.

I'm not to worry about the world, I can't change it, but I can pray for the world. We are taught to go into all the nations and baptize in the name of the Father, Son and Holy Spirit. Yes, preach the Word, Truth, and keep my head in all circumstances. Be patient with all who do not see the Truth. People come to the Truth in God's time, kairos, so be patient.

Isaiah 50:7, For the Lord GOD helps Me, Therefore, I am not disgraced; Therefore, I have set My face like flint, And I know that I will not be ashamed.

Knowing His will
Speak God's Words back to Him
Pray His Words
The only way to know His will
(heart-know)
Is through prayer

+

Luke 24:28-29, And they approached the village where they were going, and He acted as though He were going farther. But they urged Him, saying, "Stay with us, for it is getting toward evening, and the day is now nearly over." So He went in to stay with them.

The words that spoke to me from this passage are *Stay with us, nearly over, with them* and *urged Him*.

The Holy Spirit did enter the disciples when Jesus breathed into them. It was for them! To get them ready for ministry in Jesus' absence. It was revealed to others in an outward way at Pentecost.

It is easier for someone in a third world country to welcome Christ because they are already empty—they have room for Christ within them. Whereas someone in a "wealthy" country-in-comparison, like the USA, has everything and is already full with outward stuff. It's harder to empty ourselves when we are already full of stuff. But we must in order for Christ to fill us. Now, there's the challenge!

What will I do this week to grow? I will ask Christ to stay with me and to remember that the day is nearly over.

THOSE A-HA MOMENTS

Romans 8:38-39, For I am convinced that neither death, nor life, nor angels, nor principalities, nor things present, nor things to come, nor powers, nor height, nor depth, nor any other created thing, will be able to separate us from the love of God, which is in Christ Jesus our Lord.

The word that spoke to me
in this passage
is the understood word
"nothing"
Nothing can separate us
from the love of God
The only thing that can separate us
is nothing
Nothingness
The opposite of God
is nothing
If God Is the Great I AM
and God is the Way, Truth and Life
then God is True and Perfect Being
The opposite of being
is nothing
so then the opposite of True Being
is nothingness
The only thing that can separate us
is nothing
I will remember
that nothing can separate me
from the love of God
in Christ

+

Romans 5:1-2, Therefore being justified by faith, we have peace with God through our Lord Jesus Christ: By whom also we have access by faith into this grace wherein we stand, and rejoice in hope of the glory of God. (KJV)

This passage reminds me of my baptism. Baptism is the means by which we gain access to Christ. If Paul continued to talk about his unworthiness because he was Saul, then I can too because of my past. But I know that Paul was forgiven and a changed man, so I must also know that I am forgiven and a changed woman. I can rejoice in hope!

Prayer Is:
Listening
Being
Communicating
Quiet
Simple
Quantity
Love

JOURNAL-ISTS

There are many ways to journal and many journal-ists to read. One of my favorite journal-ists is Dag Hammarskjöld. He was awarded the Nobel Peace Prize in 1961. His journal is called, "Markings." His journalings include prayers, poetry, and reflections on his spiritual growth. There are many from all walks of life who could be considered journal-ists. Some include Julian of Norwich, St. Francis of Assisi, Anne Frank, Harry S. Truman and Henri Nouwen. All of them made their mark upon the world.

I could never hope to make a mark upon the world, but rather I pray that each person will be marked as Christ's own.

Your journaling will be a reflection of your life and your journey with God's guidance.

My own journaling has been varied and far between. With the help of spiritual direction, Bible studies, prayer and the guidance of the Holy Spirit I will continue to journal and see all those aha opportunities and moments.

On the left side of my journal I put a code in initials indicating what I was doing at the time. For example, next to one date I wrote "CM" which means Christian meditation. On another date I wrote "MP" which means morning prayer; and another date "SS" which means Sunday school and I wrote:

June 13th, MP:

I laugh
in my soul
about the irony
of it all

when I hear about
or read about
or talk to people
who only believe in God, the Father
and not
God: Father, Son and Holy Spirit
They don't believe in
Christ the Son
or the Spirit
and they pray, or not, to only the one as they know him
not the Three-in-One as He Is revealed

What is so funny
to me
is that their believing
in only the one
does not make it so
Father, Son and Holy Spirit
coexist
regardless of our belief in Him
God IS!
The Trinity's existence
does not depend on us
or what we believe
about the Three-in-One
But our existence
In the Trinity
does

THOSE A-HA MOMENTS

and I cry
in my soul
about the irony
of it all

November 29th, CM:

Regard not your brother's mind, but only the mind of Christ. First part, in different words from the book "The Last Lecture" by Randy Pausch. The different words and the second part from the Holy Spirit in Christian meditation. Be only concerned with God (Fr. Son, HS) and His mind. Only the cross of JC.

November 30th, SS:

Quantity is important (over quality). Spend all our time with God, it doesn't matter that we're at church, at work or at play but that we are always with Him. Just like our earthly families. We want to spend time with our parents. Our children want to spend time with us (anyway our younger children may). Our children don't always want us to be actively engaged (quality) with them. They need us to be *with* them, no matter what we are doing. Just *be with them*. Just *be with Him*. We are spiritual *be*ings.

December 1st, MP on *Luke 10:21-24*, *At that very time He rejoiced greatly in the Holy Spirit, and said, "I praise You, O Father, Lord of heaven and earth, that You have hidden these things from the wise and intelligent and have revealed them to infants. Yes, Father, for this way was well-pleasing in Your sight. All things have been handed over to Me by My Father, and no one knows who the Son is except the Father, and who the Father is except the Son, and anyone to whom the Son wills to reveal Him." Turning to the disciples, He said privately, "Blessed are the eyes which see the things you see, for I say to you, that many prophets and kings wished to see the things which you see, and did not see them, and to hear the things which you hear, and did not hear them."*

I desire to know the Father, please Son of God, Jesus, will you reveal our Father to me? I thank you for doing so through yourself and the Word, but still I desire to know God: Fr, Son & HS.

February 17th, MP:

The intercessory prayer today was asking God to accept our prayers and petitions as the first fruits of our day. I never considered my prayers in the morning as first fruits. But they are the first thing we can give to God. I also prayed that the fruits of the Spirit be given to my parents today in a special way. That they not necessarily be given these themselves (that they demonstrate joy, love, peace, patience, etc.) but that others who come into their lives demonstrate to them love, joy, peace, patience, kindness, goodness, gentleness, faithfulness and self-control. That others bring to them love, that other people are joyful around them, that others are peaceful and have patience with them. That other people around them are good and kind to them. That others are gentle, that we show our faith in them and that we possess self-control around them.

THOSE A-HA MOMENTS

March 4th, MP on *Genesis 9:11-16*, *"I establish My covenant with you; and all flesh shall never again be cut off by the water of the flood, neither shall there again be a flood to destroy the earth."* God said, *"This is the sign of the covenant which I am making between Me and you and every living creature that is with you, for all successive generations; I set My bow in the cloud, and it shall be for a sign of a covenant between Me and the earth. It shall come about, when I bring a cloud over the earth, that the bow will be seen in the cloud, and I will remember My covenant, which is between Me and you and every living creature of all flesh; and never again shall the water become a flood to destroy all flesh. When the bow is in the cloud, then I will look upon it, to remember the everlasting covenant between God and every living creature of all flesh that is on the earth."*

God promised to never again send the waters
to be a flood that destroys the whole earth
And then Jesus came
the living water to save all mankind
After the first, clouds and a bow appear
After the second (His death), dark clouds appear
and an earthquake
and the curtain tore in two
After the first, the bow divides the sky
After the second, an earthquake divides the earth
and a rip divides the curtain
After the first, light and beauty follow devastation
After the second, dark and destruction follow salvation

+

June 18th, MP:

At the beginning of morning prayer, we pray *Psalm 51:15, O Lord, open my lips, that my mouth may declare Your praise.* I've been saying this every morning for quite some time and just now realized what I was praying! I'm asking the Lord to open my lips. I'm asking for Him to open my lips, not that I open them through my own power but by the power of the Holy Spirit may they be opened. By the grace of God may they be opened. In the name of Jesus may they be opened. Help me Lord to always wait for you to open my lips to speak. Help me Lord to always let your grace be the reason I speak. Help me Lord to proclaim your praise with my words. May my words always reflect and proclaim your glory and praise. Amen! Amen! Amen!

MORE REFLECTIONS

The following are more reflections of life as a journey. Some of the poems reflect my thoughts on certain subjects. Others show the great love and respect I have for my sisters and for my parents. Other poems reflect days gone by, and yet others are light-hearted and just plain silly.

This piece explores what being in love is all about in Love Is. The lover discovers that love is not always what it seems.

Love Is

Love in days gone by was raised from scratch
maybe you both grew up together
or shared a seat on the downtown bus
then you discovered what was all the fuss.

Who knows what it is to be in love
is it a feeling of extreme like
or something we admire in a person
that fills a void or causes a fusion.

Love is finding the same interests
like reading the same splendid novels
or walking in the rain in the spring
then you know what each other can bring.

Relationships need to go somewhere
each person needs to offer something
or find the reason we're not alone
that will help explain why the love has grown.

Love is really more than offering
to loan a novel and say keep it
or saying the words we want to hear
then we may find that love is not so clear.

Passion is a long road together
which if not learned will soon wane away
or it was never at the onset
that indeed our love was at all present.

Love is many things we've all been told
but more than novels and passion deep
or words we say but we may expect
then shared love is but a common respect.

THOSE A-HA MOMENTS

Outdoor Memories is a simple poem about growing up and real-life happenings. Loving incidents are recalled with Dad and this poem is a tribute to him.

Outdoor Memories

Falling from the tree Dad
Coming to the rescue.
Bloody nose, bruised knee
Can I climb again?

Errands on a weekend
Morning chores to do
City dump, hardware store
Where else can we go?

Cities in the driveway
Playing by myself.
Little cars, lots of roads
Is it gonna rain?

Scramble up the ladder
Almost to the top.
Skin the cat, spin around
Push a little harder?

Playing with the animals
Honeybee and Calico.
Doggie's sick, call the vet
Is he coming back?

Thank you for the playhouse
Perfect every way.
Windows three, front door please
Want to join the club?

LYNNETTE GOLDY

New house, no trees
Cement driveway.
Blue specs, second grade
Do you want to play?

THOSE A-HA MOMENTS

My childhood is shared again only this time it is about being the dreaded Middle Child. I am abandoned by my older sister at the kitchen sink. I have to walk my younger sister home from school. Despite being caught between, I have learned from them both.

Middle Child

Blue rice for dinner
Mashed potato and continental
You be the golden stallion
I'll be the black.

Time to do the dishes
Please don't hide in the bathroom
You're the older one
I'm just a kid.

Writing notes in church
Youth group, choir and baptism
You be the president
I'll say the prayer.

Sixth grade, kindergarten
Started to yawn instead threw up
You're too young
I'll walk you home.

Singing to bed
Horror movies late at night
You go first
I'll turn off the light.

Movies dates stay home

LYNNETTE GOLDY

Babysit when is it my turn
You get a Nova
I ride a bike.

Love you hate you
High school college marriage kids
You are my yardsticks
I am your friend.

My two sisters and I developed a loving term for the three of us in "Sisties Ugler" (actually I think my elder sisty ugler came up with the term). We've developed stories and poems over the years. This one is just silly. I think I was hungry when I wrote it.

Sisties Ugler

Eldest sistie ugler said poetry doesn't have to rhyme. It doesn't even have to have any distinguishing characteristics, except maybe similar line rhythm, or alliteration.

She said poetry should be from the soul, reflecting feelings or emotion; not aware of sentence structure or punctuation. Famous elder sistie ugler is a great influence, so…

Three sassy sisties sought several sound systems so soon sensible sisties sorta sizzled outa sight. However, a sassy sistie resumed some sense so two sassy sisties ensued.

So, silly sensible sisties sorta sifted sourly since several societal suitors severely sat nearby. Sinning not, the silly sensible sisties on Sunday simply satiated the sordid suitors with seasoned soup.

Seven sordid suitors sardonically sent the sensible sisties a succinct summary saying how societal suitors saw the sisties as sorry sorts. Sundry surmising supplied the sisters sadly while sustaining sarcasm.

The sisties sensed senior suitors suspected a summons since salaried servers searched certain suitors' supper and found some celery.

The superiors saw a somber sight and censured the suitors. Six sentences sanctioned the suitors to the slammer and set the scene for the succeeding sitcom.

Despite the superlative sensibility of the seven societal suitors, the three sistie uglies soon sustained their singular synergy and swore to support sisters incessantly.

THOSE A-HA MOMENTS

Remembering childhood songs is something my sisters and I often have fun doing together. Songs to Live By is a result of one of those times.

Songs to Live By

Life began with dollies three
scramble up my apple tree
Didn't have a cellar door
or a rain barrel any more

Kum Bah Ya was next to learn
its hand motions show concern
Praying, crying, singing still
come by here Lord do your will

See that doggie in the window
yes the one with the pretty bow
She's just sittin' there waggin' her tail
promise me she's really for sale

Sing about the girl in love
and her sweet whisp'ring dove
Hear her heart joyfully beating
with the old hoot owl hooting

Then we'll sing a lullaby
over a rainbow in the sky
One day I'll wish I was a star
and live up with the clouds so far

Is that sunshine coming my way
I want it to be a wonderful day
Get that bluebird off my shoulder
'Fore he does what he shouldn't oughter!

The love I have for my sisters is shown in the project called Three Sisters. That love is especially described in the last stanza.

Three Sisters

Three sisters are like three characteristics
Of each of us.
I am like you, you are like me
Analogous to each other.

But yet as souls individual
As clouds above,
By God's hands made so distinctive
Each with her own wholeness.

We were born during different times.
Inherently
The production of the same parents
Singularly distinctive.

Our differences are what keeps us
All together
Calling on each others' experience
Consummates our own.

And upon glancing in the mirror
I see not me
But either the one or the other
Not entirely amazed.

Which sister is then looking back
Depends I think
On which distinguishing nature
Occupies my soul.

THOSE A-HA MOMENTS

Thank you, Mom is a tribute to my mother, written and given to her on Mother's Day.

Thank You Mom

Thank you Mom
for teaching me how to cook
to separate eggs, to double boil
to bake a cake, and mix vinegar and oil.

Thank you Mom
for teaching me how to clean
to vacuum carpets, to scrub the floor
to dust the furniture and much, much more.

Thank you Mom
for teaching me how to love
to be gentle to animals, to diaper a new baby
to clean up their mess, and give lovingly.

Thank you Mom
for giving me words and examples to live by:
"If you can't say something nice Don't say anything at all."
"Love the Lord with all your heart;
"Be Nice." and "Do unto others as you would have them do unto you."

Thank you Mom
for always loving me
even when I didn't deserve it
and for your forgiveness.

Thank you Mom
for taking care of me when I was sick

for hot tea, heating pads,
chicken soup and toast.

Thank you Mom
for taking me to tap dancing lessons,
to piano lessons and swimming lessons,
Brownie and Girl Scout meetings.

Thank you Mom for
helping me with my homework
for washing and curling my hair
and teaching me about growing up.

Thank you Mom for
taking me to church camp,
Sunday School and Church
and giving me my Christian roots.

Thank you Mom
for raising me to be what I hope
is just like you....
a loving mother.

THOSE A-HA MOMENTS

The Teacher is a tribute to our dear friend and pet dog, Max. Max lived 15 loving years and gave us much love.

My Teacher, My Friend

My teacher, my friend, met me at the door
Trash strewn from the kitchen to the couch
My teacher jumped up and licked my face
Just after he ate the tootsie roll outside
My teacher walked beside me grinning
So pleased with the bunny he caught
My teacher looked into my eyes
Pleading as he went into surgery
My teacher took his pain pills
Grateful for the few pieces of steak
This morning my teacher met me in that place
Where neither he nor I knew each other
Today my teacher is going where one day
I know he'll teach me some more
My teacher, my friend, with unconditional love
Taught me how to forgive

(Dedicated to Max — March, 1994 to March 2, 2009)

EPILOGUE

Now that you know some ways to journal, I invite you to use the opportunities that come your way. You probably won't journal every day, maybe not every week. So when there seems to be a gap in your journaling, take that as a sign of rest. For even God rested on the seventh day! But then pick up your pen, or place your fingers on that keyboard again.

A computer (especially a laptop) can be used for journaling. Computers have immense storage capacities. However, I prefer old fashioned pen and paper. The reason is not that my notebooks are smaller than most laptops.

Even though that's true. It is also true that with pen and paper I don't have to be concerned with battery power or electrical outlets or wireless connections, only running out of ink or finding a new piece of paper. But once I write in my notebook, it's there—I can't hit delete by mistake.

> I am tactile
> and the feel of a pen and the movement
> of forming the letters
> with my own hand
> seem to pull the ideas and thoughts
> right out of my head
> The pen purposely touching the paper
> followed by a quick left
> then curving slightly down

and to the right and down again
and back to the left
is music to my soul—
The letter S dances.
Crossing a T
whether it be uppercase or lowercase
or whether it be print or cursive
is completed with conviction
never experienced by pushing a button.
Sometimes
the words I'm writing speak to me more
than did the idea that put them there

Right now, I have three books I use for journaling. One is used for writing reflections from my Christian meditation, Bible reading, Sunday school, morning and evening prayer, and meetings with my spiritual director. The second book is used during our lectio divina Bible study. The third book is used for writing reflections that I glean from other books I am reading. They happen to be hardbound and were on sale. Just a simple notebook will do. I guess my Bible could also be considered my journal as there are so many written notes in the margins and comments and underlines and sticky notes and stars and exclamation points!

When you don't have your journal with you, write your thoughts on a piece of paper—whatever is available, i.e., a napkin or a receipt. Or carry a tiny notebook in your purse or pocket. Then transfer these to your journal (or tape it into your journal). Make journaling a joy!

Well, my friend, this book is coming to an end. My desire while writing this book was to inspire you, to minister to your heart, and to encourage you to journal. With that in mind, the next section of this book is for you to begin (or to re-begin) to journal your life's journey.

THOSE A-HA MOMENTS

As you journey through life, journal through every moment of your life.

Journal in prayer

Journal in worship

Journal by reflecting on:

Scripture
Work
Family
Readings
The present moment
Who the Father is
Who Christ is
Who the Holy Spirit is
Random thoughts
Words

Metaphors

Draw a picture:

Of how you feel
Of your thoughts
Of who you want to be
Of the child in you
Of the Christ in you

There are other ways of journaling that are not discussed in this book. Invent your own opportunities for journaling. What is important is that you journal as a way to recognize when the Holy Spirit is speaking to you in those aha moments, as a way to journey in your spirituality, as a way to grow in the image and likeness of God: Father, Son and Holy Spirit, as a way to find and remain in Community with Him.

**Regardless Of How We Have Lived Our Lives,
We Can Re-Turn To Him.
Write Your Prayers!
Write What God Has Given You!
See Where God Is Leading You On Your Journey With Him!
Life Is Full Of Aha Moments!**

MY JOURNEY

Dear God
Father, Son, and Holy Spirit
I pray your blessings
as I begin
a new chapter in my life
I pray your blessings
as I journal
my journey with You
Come Holy Spirit

JOURNAL

GLOSSARY

Apophatic—A theology (also known as negative theology) that recognizes that none of our attempts to describe God is adequate. He is non-describable. He is so much more than we could ever hope to describe. He is always beyond any description. Any description is negated. To be apophatic is to accept God's greatness and our understanding of Him as spiritual or mystical and not material in any sense. We cannot recognize the extent of His greatness because He is beyond our understanding. Apophatic theology spills over into other areas of our life when we recognize that faith in God is sufficient. We have no answer but God. The balance to apophatic theology is cataphatic (positive theology) when words and facts are used to understand or describe God. Thus, when we use Scripture (God's word) to understand God we are being cataphatic. When we use Christ Who Is the Word to understand God, then we are being apophatic. To put it another way: Knowing and understanding the Bible (Scripture, God's word) is the cataphatic method of understanding God. Knowing and understanding Christ (God's Word) is the apophatic method of understanding God. And yet, even this description is cataphatic.

No one has seen God at any time…. (John 1:18)

…who alone possesses immortality and dwells in unapproachable light, (1 Timothy 6:16)

Oh, the depth of the riches both of the wisdom and knowledge of God! How unsearchable are his judgments and unfathomable his ways! For who has known the mind of the Lord, or who became His counselor? For who has first given to Him that it might be paid back to Him again? For from Him and through Him and to Him are all things. To Him be the glory forever. Amen. (Romans 11:33-36)

Can you discover the depths of God? Can you discover the limits of the almighty? They are high as the heavens, what can you do? Deeper than Sheol, what can you know? (Job 11:7-8)

Chastity—From the Latin meaning pure. A chaste single person does not have sexual relations ever. The single person is pure. A chaste married person only has sexual relations with her husband and the husband only with his wife. The marriage is pure. Their marriage is a Trinity—husband, wife, and Christ.

Chrismated—Or Chrismation (sometimes called confirmation) is the Mystery by which a baptized person receives the gift of the Holy Spirit through anointing with oil. It is the initiation into the Orthodox church.

Chronos—Greek, meaning chronological, day-to-day, time as we know it. Clock or calendar time; quantitative.

Contemplation—Greek, theoria "to see God" or to be in the Presence of God; to focus on and experience exclusively the Trinitarian God.

Epiphanic—(Adjective of epiphany) — an "aha!" moment; a sudden insight into something that was seemingly ordinary.

Hubris—Pride; excessive pride; arrogance

THOSE A-HA MOMENTS

Kairos—Greek, meaning God's time; an undetermined period of time when the "aha" moments happen; when God acts in your life; as things unfold according to God's timing. Miracles happen in kairos time. Kairos time is quality time; qualitative. Example: *Mark 1:15, The time is fulfilled, and the kingdom of God is at hand.*

Lectio Divina—Latin for divine reading; a traditional Christian way to pray Scripture in order to rest in the Presence of God. Read, listen, meditate, pray, contemplate, sing and rejoice within the soul while reading God's Word.

Ruminate—The process of an animal chewing its cud quietly and slowly to break down its food and stimulate digestion. Also an ancient metaphor used as a symbol of Christians pondering the Word of God so we slowly digest (understand) it. For me, this is better than drinking from the fire hydrant.

Theosis—The process of our transformation from a "caterpillar to a butterfly," from our old self to a child of God; being transformed into Christ's likeness.

Transformation—Moving way beyond change; changing from one thing to another either immediately or over time.

CPSIA information can be obtained
at www.ICGtesting.com
Printed in the USA
LVOW12s0307111016
508256LV00001B/15/P